I0606396

PRAISE FOR *DATING DISABILITY*

"**This book is pure pleasure.** Emily doesn't just tell you a story—she welcomes you into her world with such radiant honesty and wit that you forget you're reading at all. You're not just observing; you're living it with her.

By the final page, one truth becomes unshakably clear: **Love is your birthright.**

No matter what stories you've told to disqualify yourself from intimacy, you can set them down. You can show up, open up, and create the wild, tender, epic love you deserve.

Emily is living proof. And through this brilliant, bold, and beautiful book, she reminds us that no matter how daunting the challenge, we never, ever give up on love."

—LONDIN ANGEL WINTERS, coauthor of *Playing With Fire: The Spiritual Path of Intimate Relationship*

"Emily's brave storytelling of her intimate dreams, crushes, and heartaches are devastatingly relatable. You'll laugh, you'll cry; because you've been there too. But it's so much more than a story. The point of *Dating Disability* is to help you examine how your own physical and emotional wounds, your visible and invisible traumas, are stored in your body."

—STEVEN HUANG, perennially disillusioned dater

"Emily is refreshingly candid and forthright as she navigates the delightful and baffling moments of moving as an atypical body through a conventional body-centric world. This book is a validating and edifying read for anyone—disabled or non-disabled—who is fearless enough to take the plunge and seek an intimate connection with another, regardless of the interpersonal roller coaster it can be. Emily's self-aware insights are a model in resisting shame, moving at one's own pace, and finding the opportunities for confidence-building along the way."

—REGAN LINTON, MSW, MFA, playwright, director, and disability advocate

"In emotionally raw and candid stories that map her journey from childhood through to adulthood, Emily Goodson's sharp, funny gaze is turned toward her own romantic life. *Dating Disability* is a necessary debut that speaks to everyone, while justifiably centering differently abled perspectives. Emily's perspective on disability and dating is a much needed one, as this topic isn't discussed as often, openly, or freely as it should be. Emily's voice is a welcome new addition to our wider movement of advocacy."

—JENNEH RISHE, BSN, RN, founder of The Endometriosis Coalition and author of *Part of You, Not All of You*

"Swipe right on *Dating Disability*. Emily Goodson's moving and powerfully vulnerable memoir is unflinchingly honest and beautifully written. Prepare to fall in love with Emily and her storytelling."

—RANDI BRAUN, *Wall Street Journal* bestselling author of *Something Major: The New Playbook for Women at Work*

"Shame thinks it keeps us safe, but it hides the things that heal us. Emily Goodson is shame's living rebuke. Through force of personality, this book rips into shame, recounting the author's brave journey out of physical bondage and psychological imprisonment with rare candor. Not with platitudes and a face mask, but an on-the-nose real-life story of the sexual urge put down, thwarted, and resurrected back to life."

—MICHAEL APPLETON, senior psychotherapist in child and adult services

DATING DIS ABILITY

15 STORIES OF DEALING WITH THE BS AND BUILDING CONFIDENCE

EMILY GOODSON

www.amplifypublishinggroup.com

Dating Disability: 15 Stories of Dealing with the BS and Building Confidence

Second Printing. This Amplify Publishing edition printed in 2026.

For more information, please contact:
Amplify Publishing, an imprint of Amplify Publishing Group
620 Herndon Parkway, Suite 220
Herndon, VA 20170
info@amplifypublishing.com

Library of Congress Control Number: 2025909900

CPSIA Code: PRV0126B

ISBN-13: 979-8-89138-640-2

Printed in the United States

To my instructors, fellow riders, and the studio crew at SoulCycle NoMad—I love all of you and have grown immensely because of your presence in my life. Thank you for pushing me to be 1% better every day.

CONTENTS

PART TWO: FACING THE GREMLINS

TAKEAWAYS

FOREWORD

SOME THURSDAY NIGHT IN JUNE OF 2014, I was sitting at a bar in Washington, D.C., a little bowl of goldfish and a generous pour of sauv blanc in front of me. As I chatted with the bartender, a tall man with luscious, dark hair walked behind me and sat two stools down. I mean, have mercy, this guy's hair rivaled Uncle Jesse's from *Full House*.

Eventually, the fried shrimp I ordered arrived and, by this point, John Stamos and I had struck up a conversation. We talked of traveling to Europe, music, and college football while he sipped his bourbon rocks, and I dunked my shrimp in ketchup. He was stylish, knowledgeable, fun, and lived in my neighborhood. All green lights.

Yet, there was one massive problem.

He had yet to see me stand up and walk, and I was terrified of what he would think when I did.

When I was eight years old, I became partially paralyzed on the left side of my body. I became physically disabled. A clump of blood vessels (also called a vascular malformation) started bleeding in my brain stem. At first the bleeding went nefariously unnoticed, and then suddenly, the onset of my partial paralysis.

In a matter of hours, I started limping and couldn't raise my left arm to so much as push an elevator button. My left hand had been able to throw a pretty impressive curveball that morning, and suddenly I couldn't even open it.

A week after the doctors discovered the malformation and stopped the harmful bleeding, I underwent brain surgery to remove the clump (out of fear it would bleed again). The surgeons carefully cut four millimeters into the back, right side of my head, removed what they needed, and stitched me back up.

When I emerged from surgery, I was even weaker on my left side—only slightly able to flex my left arm in response to painful stimuli. I tried to verbalize my fears and questions, but no words came out. I was able to cry, though, which I did a lot.

The doctors were shocked. They had not operated anywhere near my speech center and didn't anticipate a loss of speech.

So, while they spent their days researching potential reasons for my muted existence, I sat in the hospital bed frustratedly trying to communicate by pointing to alphabet letters on a cardboard pad. The more I tried to communicate, the more I failed. My hurried and anxious pointing was too rapid for anyone to follow and piece together. So, I remained locked in my own head, hopeless and despondent.

Fast forward a few months.

My speech returned with therapy. Also with therapy, I relearned how to walk—though with an altered gait—and to perform daily tasks with the use of one hand and one arm. I was (and am) very lucky.

The physical effects of my brain injury were significant, and yet, adapting to them didn't prove to be the greatest challenge of my life.

That honor was reserved for my emotional landscape. That's where the biggest cuts were, and if I'm being honest, those are the cuts I'm still working to heal.

My childhood frustration at my inability to communicate through an alphabetic letterboard would eventually repeat itself in a failure to communicate what I wanted from intimate relationships as an adult. My struggle to express my interiority, my desires, and what I knew I deserved growing up became an immense shame that was paralyzing in its own right. For decades I longed to date, to be someone's girlfriend, but I could never even make it to first base.

And that experience was far more painful to me than my physicality ever was.

The good news, though, is I didn't stay in that painful emotional state.

I learned to navigate the BS—the emotions, the lack of representation, the stereotypes, all of it—and have more confidence in myself.

That process was not easy or quick. And *that* is this story.

INTRODUCTION

Chapter 1

I'M A DISABLED WOMAN. IS THAT A DATING DEAL-BREAKER?

"I'M A DISABLED WOMAN. Is that a dating deal-breaker?" This is not only the title of a column I wrote and published in the *Los Angeles Times* in 2022, but a question I asked myself daily growing up as a teenager in Virginia, a college student in North Carolina, and a young adult in Washington, D.C.

I spent my young adult years in Washington, D.C., not getting anywhere close to having that boyfriend I so desperately wanted. Instead, the aforementioned bar fear ran through my head on a weekly basis.

As I entered my thirties—still single and celibate—the hard truth I eventually had to face was that I—not the men I was interested in—made my physical disability a dating deal-breaker.

This book is the story of why I viewed physical disability as one of my deal-breakers (let's be honest, the primary one) and how I moved beyond that way of thinking to build greater confidence in myself.

We all consider parts of our identity to be deal-breakers at some point—no matter whether we are disabled or non-disabled. I had thought I was alone in feeling that way, but I now know that I wasn't.

At some point in our lives, we all have pieces of ourselves that we are afraid will be judged if we own them and live them out loud. We all fear that if we share our full selves, we will be shamed for who we are or, perhaps worse, stereotyped—put into rigid boxes we don't want to be in and that certainly do not tell our full stories. For me, the dating deal-breakers I perceived as my own were my physical disability and my lack of sexual experience with a partner.

Maybe you have also considered those things your deal-breakers. Maybe not. Regardless, we all perceive something about ourselves to be a deal-breaker because of the stories society tells us and how we internalize those stories.

For that reason, *this* story is here to help all of us—those with disabilities, parents of children with disabilities, those in relationships, those who are temporarily disabled because of a surgery or illness or accident, and even those haters who think this story isn't necessary.

This story is important because we have all been negatively affected by dominant, prejudicial societal narratives. None of us should consider parts of ourselves deal-breakers to being loved, and yet we do.

So, let's get moving, figure out how to confront that BS and be more confident, shall we?

Chapter 2

SOME FRAMING

PART 1 OF THIS BOOK FOCUSES on my childhood and young adult years, stories of how and why I developed an unhealthy inner narrative around my disability and sexuality. And Part 2 tells the stories of how I busted out of that narrative to build more confidence and self-worth.

I invite you to read each story, digest it, and reflect on the ways it speaks to you and your own personal experience—whatever that includes.

At the end of Part 2, you'll find takeaways for various readers. I've limited sharing my learnings in the earlier chapters to allow you to form your own thoughts. Given that, you will find a nice collection of my reflections at the end of the book.

As we get started, let's discuss three things.

1. What Is Disability?

For some of you who have life experience with disability, this part may be a bit rote. But in the spirit of inclusion—because isn't that at the core of this book's message!—I'll lay it out for all. Disability is difference. Differences in how people move, communicate, think, and operate in the world.

People with disabilities adapt on a daily, and often hourly, basis. We use different tools and strategies than non-disabled people may use because most of the world's systems were not designed for us.

People with disabilities are not a monolith.

Not everyone in the disability community has an apparent disability, like I do. When you meet me in person and see me walk, you can tell I have a physical disability. However, many people out there identify as disabled, but we can't perceive their disability when meeting them or talking to them.

People who identify as disabled are a multiplicity. People with disabilities belong to all sexual orientations, ages, races, religions, and socioeconomic classes.

Some disabilities come in the form of chronic illness. Some include a learning, emotional, or intellectual difference. Some people are born with their disability and some start to experience disability later in life.

My perspective in this book largely speaks to my story as a cis, white woman with a physical disability living in the United States. Mine is a valuable perspective to consider, but so is that of someone with a disability who has a different experience than I do. By all means, read on, but as you do, please also consider—or continue—consulting a breadth of perspectives by other subject matter experts. Whether book, article, movie, podcast, etc., there are many resources to tap, and I've listed a good few on a website linked in the Takeaways section.

2. What About Language?

You'll notice in this book that I refer to myself as a "woman with a disability" or a "person with a disability." This language structure is called person-first. Some people prefer to identify as a "disabled person," which is identity-first language. Still others with disabilities are happy to be referenced in either framework or use completely different language depending on their geography.

None of these structures or preferences are inherently right or wrong. However, what's important is to pay attention (and ask, if needed) to personal preference.

3. What About All These Men?

Many of my crushes and dates will be mentioned in this book. Yes, there are A LOT of them. As a roommate once reflected to me, "You've always loved having a crush."

She wasn't wrong. I love my crushes, my coffee, and my indoor cycling. At this point, I doubt any of that will ever stop.

I am truly grateful to every single man I have been on a date with and am particularly grateful to those who didn't reciprocate the same romantic feelings I felt for them. I have learned and grown a tremendous amount because of the mirrors they were to me.

As you read this book, please treat the current and former men in my life with the same respect and love.

Many of them were extremely patient with me

when I didn't have the tools to help myself or communicate what I wanted.

So, as you read the various failed sexcapades, please do it lovingly—like I do.

With all of that said, let's get into my banana debacle (I said what I said) and my subsequent path to build greater confidence.

PART ONE

THE BANANA AND OTHER DEBACLES

Chapter 1

THE FIRST BRICK IN THE WALL

When I was thirteen, I went on my first trip to California with my family. One of the stops on that trip was Yosemite National Park.

Two big things happened at Yosemite. Sadly, no, I didn't spot a bear.

However, I did experience my first spotting (that means I got my period) and, less exciting, I sprained my left wrist.

After my brain surgery, my physical therapist attempted to teach me how to fall in a way that wouldn't injure my weaker wrist.

Each week at physical therapy, I would kneel on the ground, with my back straight up, and brace myself for a shove I knew was imminent. The physical therapist, standing behind me, would then push me forward when I least expected it to train me to land on my stronger, right forearm. If I incorrectly landed on my weaker, left forearm, back I went into position for the PT (physical therapist) to push me down again.

Unfortunately, the PT's shoving and training method wasn't 100 percent effective. At some point on a hike through Yosemite five years later, I fell, and landed on my weaker, left wrist.

After the fall, I walked back to the hotel by myself clutching my left arm, the pain radiating and stinging from my wrist up to my elbow. I limped through the hotel entrance full of families hugging each other around glowing fire pits, when suddenly another, stronger pain took over.

I noticed people were staring at me.

Were they staring at me because I was crying and holding my arm, clearly in pain? Or were they staring at me because I walked with a pronounced limp? Or both?

The why behind their stares became the *only* thing I could think about.

I swallowed against the huge lump in my throat as I determined they probably weren't staring at me because I was crying. And that infuriated me. I was boiling hot—and not because of the fire pits. Tears ran faster down my face.

Looking back on that young girl, I feel so much compassion for what she carried in that moment. I know that what caused her embarrassment and anger was not the stares, but the story those stares told her about her worth. It was the overwhelm of not knowing how to emotionally handle what was going on inside of her and not being told what a gift it was to be different.

I grew up in the 1990s, a product of where I lived, the family I was born to, and the general stigma around mental health at the time. As a result, I didn't go to talk therapy or cognitive behavioral therapy after my brain surgery. I only attended speech and physical therapy. No one knew at the time that my internal self—not my physical body—needed the most healing and direction post-injury. But she did.

Without a therapist, coach, or even a role model with a physical disability, I didn't have an outlet for exploring my emotions and differences, and thus they overwhelmed me. Yosemite was just the start.

When I realized the overwhelm was happening, I employed the best coping strategy I could figure out: walls. Starting at those fire pits, I built emotional walls, brick by brick, inside of me so people's stares wouldn't upset me. Walls that were as hard as steel so others couldn't penetrate. Walls that were there to hold in my anger over the stories the stares told me.

I had already experienced so much physical and emotional pain in my life, being separated from my family and friends in hospitals, that I didn't want any more. The walls (so I thought) would solve that.

What I didn't anticipate, though (and would find out a decade later), was that those walls would also become my enemy. They would grow to inhibit my ability to communicate my positive wants, desires, and feelings—including those for romance and sex. They would prevent me from having the intimate relationships I would desire as a teenager.

Ignorant to the consequences, up went my internal walls at Yosemite so I didn't have to make sense of what the staring meant. And, as I returned to my life and middle school in Virginia, they accompanied me.

Chapter 2

THE MIDDLE SCHOOL DANCE

My romantic interest in boys piqued about the same time as the trip to Yosemite.

I crushed on several boys in my middle school classes. I also had a very visceral, turned-on response to Daniel Day-Lewis's John Proctor in the 1996 movie version of *The Crucible*. That "give me my name" scene still does it for me today … yellow rotten teeth and all.

My middle school was a new school with new people. I didn't feel like one of the popular students, but I had a small group of friends and enjoyed my classes (with the very notable exception of math).

I was also one of only two students in the entire school with an apparent disability.

In middle school, I became self-conscious because I realized that my peers and teachers treated me differently. I didn't want people to treat me differently. Or perhaps it's most accurate to say that I didn't want boys to treat me differently. And I started to notice that they did.

My middle school hosted Saturday night dances in the cafeteria. Before these dances, I would sit in front of my bedroom mirror and apply *at least* three layers of anti-perspirant, desperate to ensure no one would see a drop of sweat on my dress.

On one particular Saturday night, I gathered with the other girls in the bathroom before the dance started. My friends and I giggled together. I was excited about the potential of my crush asking me to dance. Could that *possibly* happen?

As we all stood at the sinks primping our hair, one of the girls stepped toward me to whisper that my crush wanted to dance with me. I turned to my best friend and gasped. I couldn't believe it. My dreams were coming true.

I very quickly applied more Dr. Pepper lip gloss—just in case a kiss was coming!

When I walked through the cafeteria doors, lights twinkling above me, the Red Sea of people parted as if on cue and my crush stepped forward to ask me to dance. Just like in all the movies I had seen. It was glorious.

Dancing at that time consisted of standing three feet apart with my arms around this guy's neck and his hands slightly above my waist. So that's what we did.

We swayed back and forth, eyes locked on each other for three minutes. I was happy he wasn't six feet tall so both of my arms could comfortably encircle his neck. It was perfect. But then all of a sudden, the music ended. We stared at each other awkwardly for a nanosecond and quickly scampered back to our respective corners of the room.

And that was that.

No kiss, no follow-up dance, no holding hands, or debriefing bathroom giggles. On Monday, it was business as usual at the schoolhouse.

I was confused. I liked this boy. I was told that he liked me. He asked me to dance. But why didn't he kiss me or walk me outside to the football field? We were right on the cusp of being boyfriend and girlfriend, but why didn't we get there?

My brain did its best to connect the dots between my questions and reality—it must be because I walk differently, and he doesn't like that.

That must be it. OK, we've (my brain and I) decided. No more questions or wondering needed.

So, onward I went toward high school, still in hopes of receiving a first kiss but also subconsciously starting to blame my body for why that kiss wasn't happening.

Chapter 3

THE DREADED BANANA

GROWING UP, I pushed through the frustration I felt being unable to tie tennis shoes or ride a bicycle outdoors—things I had done before my injury. Physically, I exhausted myself expending more energy daily than a non-disabled person does. I learned to dress with one functional hand, learned to carry all my school books to class with one strong arm, and tried to utilize muscles that were frozen to propel myself back up when I fell.

Dating-wise, guys weren't asking me to dances, but I wasn't asking them either—unless motivated by excessive friendly encouragement from a friend and her mother. Also known as, "Go upstairs, call him, and don't come back down until you do."

In not verbalizing those desires and feelings, I was keeping myself safe. *Problem solved*, I thought. Nothing could affect me.

And yet, I was about to confront a new reality I hadn't even begun to consider. And it involved bananas.

Freshman year of high school, my classmates and I were ushered out of our school building and into some mobile trailers behind the gym.

Can you guess where this is going? The subject that is *so* awkward it had to be banished outside the building.

Yes, that's right. Sex ed.

We sat in a mobile trailer week after week, watched *The Karen Carpenter Story*, discussed unwanted pregnancies, learned about AIDS, and ... were instructed on how to put a condom on a banana.

By this point, I knew I wanted to have sex with men. That was clear from watching *Titanic* and frequently replaying the part where Leonardo DiCaprio's Jack makes love to Kate Winslet's Rose.

My main problem, or so I thought, was that no Jack at school seemed to want me as his Rose. All the

Jacks just wanted to be my friend.

And now sex ed taught me that I had a new problem.

Condoms in shiny wrappers were passed out the first day of class. I sat at my desk, awkwardly looking around to figure out what to do. At first, I was unable to even open the condom packaging with one hand. There was no tearing that top open with my normal tricks.

I tried with my teeth to no avail. Scissors would have to be involved. Everyone's dream equipment in an intimate, sexual moment.

What was I going to do?

How do I hold the banana and unroll the condom at the same time with only one hand? It was a terrible conundrum.

I watched as my classmates successfully adorned their bananas.

If I ever managed to get the packaging open, I thought I could unroll the condom with one hand when the banana was not involved. But didn't the banana have to be involved? There were so many questions and no answers.

As I watched others, I observed that when the banana was present, you definitely had to have two hands to put a condom on with any kind of speed. And, based on what I had heard, speed (unlike the scissors) seemed to be a desired thing in these situations.

My anxiety burned hotter.

Fast forward a few decades—when I actually needed this information. I was hooking up with a guy who was literally on top of me when he brought up the dreaded topic: condoms. When I said that yes, a condom would be useful, he quickly (as I expected to be the case) reached for the side table drawer, opened the wrapper, and put it on himself.

I was furious. But not at him—at my sex ed teachers. Why did I have to awkwardly sit through the banana lessons if I wasn't expected to put the condom on someone? Why didn't anyone tell fifteen-year-old Emily this and save her the anxiety?

Looking back, I now know that the need to tell fifteen-year-old Emily this never occurred to my sex ed teachers. They never considered the discussion because they were non-disabled and not taught to accommodate anything different. My school's U.S. history class didn't go into any kind of detail on FDR and polio or the fight for Section 504. So, a more inclusive sex ed class definitely wasn't on their radar.

And that lack of relevant education was harmful to me.

The internal walls I built growing up were only part of my problem. The lack of conversations in the public sphere about disability and intimacy further amplified an internal monologue that screamed I wasn't worthy—that I was right to feel invisible. And because of the lack of conversation, my own narrative was encouraged to run rampant and unchecked, leaving me without the skills to be ready for my Leonardo DiCaprio—whomever he might be.

Let's just say, sex ed classes did me no favors.

Chapter 4

"YOU CAN'T GO TO MEXICO"

I WAS NOT A FAN OF MY SEX ED CLASS in high school; however, I did have more fulfilling classes. For instance, my Spanish classes.

I started taking Spanish in the sixth grade and loved it.

A few years later, I had become pretty proficient. And, for the first time ever, one of my teachers announced that they planned to take a student group to Mexico to see the wonders of the Aztec and Mayan cultures and immerse us in the language we had been studying.

I desperately wanted to go. A friend at the time had already been to Mexico several times with her family and I was immensely jealous. This was my chance to have the same experience and put my language skills to the test.

I attended the trip information session with my parents, excited at the thought of going to a foreign country with my friends—and without my family. My parents and I sat in the classroom and saw pictures of the gorgeous pyramids built by the ancients at Teotihuacán. I was amazed at the prehistoric architecture and wondered what mysteries it held.

My excitement was, sadly, short-lived.

After the information session ended, my mother pulled me aside.

"Emily," she said, "you can't go on this trip." My throat tightened.

When I asked why, she said, "Because what if you climb a pyramid and aren't able to get back down?"

Gut punch. While I had been marveling at the size and scale of history, my mother had been studying the lack of handrails on the stairs.

At the time, I wore various arm splints to try and improve my mobility. Some of them were quite painful and restrictive. I would literally unhook one of them in my sleep. I would wake up at 8:00 a.m. and it would be on the ground, having been thrown there by a half-awake Emily at 3:00 a.m.

As my mother spoke, I thought of that brace. I wanted to do the exact same thing to her at that moment.

She had overtly told me I couldn't do something that I wanted to do because of my physical differences. Up until this point, I *told myself* that my lack of a boyfriend existed because I was different. But now I was specifically told by someone else that I couldn't have an experience I wanted because of my body. Ouch.

Now, with respect to my mother, I will tell you that I have since been to Mexico and Teotihuacán.

Of course, I saw the lack of handrails and steep inclines and didn't think they would be a problem. So, I charged up the first twenty stairs of a Teotihuacán platform with excitement.

I made it to the top, glanced around at the massive scale of the entire situation, and was in awe. I then walked to the edge of the platform to go down into the courtyard and thought, *Oh shit, what am I going to do now? Has my mother's proclamation come true?*

The lack of handrails might be a challenge.

As it turned out though, my mom should not have been worried. Why? Because a stranger named David, who hailed from Utah, saw me playing out different scenarios in my head and graciously offered me his arm to descend the stairs.

Afterward, I attempted a second pyramid only to find it had no David at the top. I ended up scooting back down on my butt, step by step, and from there I decided I'd had enough climbing without a David in tow. But still. I'd climbed up and gotten down. And that was something.

The difference between taking myself to Teotihuacán in 2022 and my mother's "no" from childhood is that the debacle was of *my* choosing.

I wasn't barred from doing something because I was different. I climbed those pyramids the best I could, safely. I didn't climb all of them, but I was there. I saw them. I experienced something.

When high school Emily stood in that hallway, furious at her mother, she didn't know she would make it to Mexico twenty years later, but she was hopeful about a different light at the end of the tunnel of anger: college.

Chapter 5

I DID NOT LIKE THAT THERAPIST

I WENT TO COLLEGE IN NORTH CAROLINA. At least twelve of my high school classmates went to the same university in Virginia, but I shipped off to dear old Wake Forest all by myself.

I had an amazing experience at Wake Forest. I made great friends; I giggled anytime I saw the current NBA player, Chris Paul, who was in my same class year; and I gasped in awe when the great Dr. Maya Angelou, who taught there at the time, passed me on the quad. It was a wonderful four years where I devoted myself to studying literature and educational philosophy.

All of the emotional pain and yuckiness you just

read about from my middle and high school years? I know you're hoping it disappeared, right? Now that I was on my own and not being taught to fall a certain way or told I couldn't go to Mexico?

Sadly, no. It didn't go away. Those little gremlins followed me to college.

One thing did change though—the normal, internal walls around my pain started to become ineffective.

Within the first few months of freshman year, I told a friend about my lack of sexual experience, hoping for some comfort and answers. Instead, I was met with a look of pity followed by, "Well, when it happens, you don't have to tell him it's your first time."

Her remark resurfaced a lot of sad, angry feelings and I tried to push them all the way down into the soles of my shoes, just like in high school.

But something didn't work this time. After the initial excitement of college faded and nothing changed romantically (despite my hopes for the cute guy at orientation), my repressed feelings got the better of me. I started to cry a lot at night. I cried over the new guy friends I met who I wished saw me romantically. I cried when people in my shared living spaces disagreed with me or raised their voices at me for rather mundane reasons. I cried because I was emotionally overwhelmed, and the emotions needed to get out.

As the time at Wake Forest went on, I became more familiar with the idea of therapy. A friend of mine reported that the on-campus center was really helping them deal with their own stuff. At first, I rejected the idea of going. I was terrified that my parents would see a charge for therapy on their tuition bill, ask about it, and I would have to explain.

But eventually, I bit the bullet and off to the on-campus mental health therapist I went. I figured it was worth a try. Perhaps they could help change my dating circumstances if nothing else.

"What brings you here today?" asked the therapist. I responded that a guy didn't seem to be interested in me as anything more than a friend. That he'd ask me to hang out at Panera all the time, and he'd call and text regularly. All normal signs of wanting to get to know someone romantically. So why hadn't we kissed? I told the therapist I didn't understand why this guy wasn't interested in a romantic relationship.

The therapist nodded. "How does that make you feel?" he asked.

"Angry," I said. "Because no one has *ever* wanted to date me or be with me romantically."

I barely managed to get the words out of my mouth before the sobs started and big tears rolled down my face.

We sat and stared at each other in silence. I was expecting some sympathy or the usual adage: "When you least expect it, you'll meet the right person." Snore.

Instead, to my horror, the therapist asked, "Why are you covering your face and looking down when you cry?"

What started as a steady trickle of tears then turned to a waterfall. His question made me cry more. He had hit a core wound.

I didn't tell him, but there were many times as a child and young adult, including once at a funeral, where I was told not to cry in public.

The therapist uncovered that I had internalized the belief that crying was bad and so covered my face when doing it. Yet another way I restricted my emotions—just like the internal walls I built at Yosemite.

These behaviors were impeding my ability to date because I wasn't capable of effectively communicating feelings or desires. I wasn't ready to make that connection at the time, though. I felt attacked by this therapist. I wanted help getting laid and this guy was asking me why I covered my face when crying. I thought he was missing the plot. (In reality, I was the one missing the plot, but more on that later.)

As you might guess, I didn't see that therapist again. There were too many hard emotions and unraveling layers. It takes an immense amount of courage to venture into a decades-deep well of unworthiness. And I wasn't there yet. Even though I was starting to sense that the shame and discomfort I felt were circling the drain of my emotional issues, I wasn't ready to acknowledge that. I also didn't have all the people and tools I needed to feel safe enough to explore.

So, I said goodbye to the therapist and dove back into the safe, objective space of my collegiate studies and work.

And even though I didn't find this therapy visit successful at the time, I realize in looking back that it was the start of me building more confidence in myself and owning my emotions. While I wouldn't really approach these issues again for years to come, some bricks in my internal walls did crack with the therapist's powerful question. And thus began the most important process of my life.

Chapter 6

CHASING THE OYSTER BAR GUY

After college I stayed and worked in North Carolina for a few years. As all my friends quickly partnered up and got married, though, I decided it was time for a change and moved to Washington, D.C., where I discovered a fabulous chain of oyster bars named Hank's. I spent the majority of my mid-to-late-twenties in one Hank or another *(ba dum tss).* My birthday, New Year's Eve, any given Sunday—you could find me at Hank's.

One of the restaurant locations had theme nights and played movies on TVs above the bar. They had a night for *Top Gun*, *Super Mario Bros.*, and even took my suggestion to host a night for *The Sandlot*. Though

I barely got to enjoy my own suggestion because I skipped out after an hour to meet a guy whose band was playing at a house party. (I know—it's despicable behavior. But we all make mistakes when pursuing our goals and, ideally, we grow from them. I know I have.)

One Sunday, one of the men I met in our Hank's circle accidentally bought my cocktails and fried shrimp. We met at the bar and started flirting. When he asked for his check, the bartender assumed we were together and gave this guy both his bill and mine, which he promptly paid without complaint and left.

I ran into this guy probably once a month over the course of the next year. Most likely because I visited that bar at the exact same time every Sunday hoping to run into him (but that's beside the point). The point is that he eventually got the message and suggested we intentionally meet at that bar the next weekend.

I was so excited. My efforts were paying off.

I showed up the next weekend all glammed up and ready to go ... and he didn't.

It should have been a red blinking light about his level of interest in me. But, of course, I didn't see it that way and gave him another chance.

The casual flirting continued via text and one Saturday night he invited me over to his house to watch a movie. I immediately ran to my mirror to adjust my clothes and makeup. I texted him back to confirm I was interested in coming over and asked for his address.

And then nothing. He ghosted. No response. And I never saw him again.

One would think I could have at least gotten a kiss for all my trouble chasing him around for a year. But alas, no. He never followed up on that text and I didn't attempt to call or clarify.

Now, even though I didn't score any bases that night, it was still important. I was officially chipping away at the negative self-talk and systemic issues that had plagued me for so long. In that moment, I gained a greater willingness to pursue what I wanted. I may not have been fully actualized, but I kept showing up at the bar for a year. And, as a result, I had gotten further toward my goals than ever before.

Up until that point, I had been asked to go as an escort to college dances and parties, but I had certainly never been asked to come over to someone's house at 11:00 p.m. to watch a movie. That was a big first for a little girl who had grown up in a culture that desexualizes, infantilizes, and marginalizes people with disabilities. That was also a big first for a little girl who didn't want to show any emotions or vulnerability.

And my confidence in my desires and in what I deserved kept building.

Chapter 7

TWO STEPS FORWARD, ONE STEP BACK

It was a breezy summer night in rural North Carolina. I was in my late twenties. Some friends and I were at a winery listening to jazz music.

At some point, as conversations amongst single people almost always do, the dialogue turned toward dating.

As I shared my continued frustration with dating and how no men seemed to be interested in having sex with me, a friend leaned in and, in a drunken, misguided attempt at logic, said, "You will probably never get married because no one marries a disabled person."

Ugh. My big ugly internal monologue mirrored

back at me. Marriage: another experience I wasn't allowed to have.

I proceeded to drink more wine than I had ever drunk in my life.

An hour later, I threw up in the car on the way back to our hotel. When we arrived, I struggled to get out of the car and then threw up again before I was put to bed by one of my friends. I woke up multiple times that night, in and out of consciousness, crying and proclaiming my utter embarrassment as a friend sat with me and tried to soothe me.

I couldn't be soothed. I was overwhelmed hearing my own inner fears and the world's stereotypes mirrored back to me.

I can't blame the person who declared me unmarriable, because it's the same statement I told myself and the same one society and the media still sometimes convey. That person was a mouthpiece for public consensus, and I didn't have the strength or the knowledge to correct the message. Instead, I tried to drink the hurt away.

I felt like I was back to square one. Forget all my progress with the Oyster Bar Guy. All my dating hopes had been dashed again.

In my twenties, my dating journey was two steps forward and one massive step back.

This winery expedition? Definitely a step back in my quest to build self-worth. However, even though I didn't see the connection at the time, I was taking two steps forward through other channels—specifically, in my discovery of the wonderful world of professional coaching.

In my twenties, I worked in human resources leadership for various tech start-ups. As part of these jobs, I studied with professional leadership coaches one-on-one. We would meet once a week for an hour, in-person or over the phone, to talk about the challenges I was having at work, such as feedback I had received or feedback I needed to give.

At one point, one of my teams also did a group engagement where we had a coaching cohort observe our weekly meetings and interactions. I started to fall in love with the skill set and even obtained several coaching certifications so I could work with employees more effectively.

I didn't seek out this coaching training previously

because I didn't know it existed. However, once I encountered it, I started to see the benefits pretty quickly. I learned about self-awareness. I learned about triggers. And I learned about the need to stand up for myself.

And while I couldn't do that on the winery trip, I was gaining the skills I needed to self-advocate shortly thereafter in both personal and professional circumstances. Through coaching, I would start to build the tools I needed to be confident in sharing my opinions and experiences, no matter what society or others threw at me.

Chapter 8

FIRST TIMES ARE A BIG DEAL

THE FOLLOWING SPRING, I ended up drinking beers with a guy after going to a sporting event. He was friends with some of my friends. We had all been attending a professional match and afterward migrated to the local watering hole. Most people huddled in a booth in the corner, but I eyed this guy right when we walked in and lingered at the bar as he ordered beers.

He approached me and we ended up on bar stools, just the two of us, talking. An hour quickly passed by and, at some point, cars were called for our overserved friends in the booth.

As our friends departed, we stayed on those stools and chatted about our love of baseball and random trivia. I thought he was really cute and funny. I also loved his great head of hair.

Eventually though, much to my dismay, I had to dash across the street to meet some other friends for dinner.

Admittedly, I was self-conscious about what he would think when he saw me get up and leave to walk across the street. But he had already asked for my number and texted me his. I had at least managed not to strike out. He did seem interested.

So, I got up to go to dinner, thinking, *Maybe he won't notice. Maybe he won't care.* Regardless, I knew I could always text him.

I left the bar, didn't look back, and hurried across the street to my friends. I sat down—a bit late because, you know, priorities—across from a college friend and her husband.

As we chatted, my phone chirped. I saw the number and squealed. The man of the moment had texted to say it was nice to meet me and we should go to dinner sometime. I was beaming. This time, it was really game on.

Some texting and meetups ensued. He would come

to meet my friends and me out at baseball games or restaurants—the usual thing. We never went to dinner, just the two of us, but I didn't care. I was enjoying the casual attachment. It suited my level of development.

One Saturday night a few weeks later, with my roommate out of town, I was enjoying the apartment and television by myself in a T-shirt and glasses.

As I watched a Meg Ryan romantic comedy, my phone buzzed. It was my Baseball Guy at 10:00 p.m., asking where I was. I knew where this was headed, and this time, I got his address. Green light.

I ran to the bathroom and swapped my glasses for contacts. I stayed in my baseball jersey T-shirt and jeans because, you know, it was on-brand.

I took an Uber to his house. When I got there, he took me on a tour of the kitchen, backyard, living room, and eventually upstairs to his bedroom. I was excited, but mostly I was very unsure of how to approach what was about to happen. Was this tour thing normal?

I stood in the doorframe to his bedroom. He stood about five feet away in the room and we awkwardly chatted for a solid two minutes.

Then, there was a long pause before he bounded over to the doorframe, grabbed my arms, and asked, "Why are you so hesitant?" before kissing me.

Why are you so hesitant? He had no idea.

I didn't realize I looked hesitant externally, but I certainly felt it inside. Even though I fully consented to what was about to happen—emotionally and physically I was engaging in something completely new. This was my first kiss—after decades of waiting and listening to countless sex stories from others—my moment had *at last* arrived. This was a big deal for me, even if it was a regular Saturday night for him.

I should have stopped right there and told him about my lack of experience, but I didn't. I didn't have the skills to bring up my lack of history and discomfort with it. The two of us had never even touched on my physical disability in prior interactions. He didn't ask and I didn't volunteer. I think the old (bad) advice, "You don't have to tell him..." lingered in my mind on all fronts. So, onward we went.

Making out that night was lovely. He also completely respected my decision not to spend the night.

We fooled around one more time that month before things fizzled. Neither of us pursued anything formal. I didn't attempt to initiate a conversation about our status, which perhaps should have indicated to me that I still had work to do on the skills needed for a serious relationship. But I was happy and didn't want to dig deep.

So, what happened next? Did I take that next step to gain the skills I needed? Did I meet the next guy and finally claim that "girlfriend" label I desired so much?

No.

As many of you know, change doesn't happen that quickly. And, I still had work to do on sharing all the parts of me I had kept hidden for so long.

But all of that aside, I had had a major "first." A first kiss and several make-out sessions to boot.

Several years went by after Baseball Guy—years that proved I was still partially stuck in my same friend-zone patterns, struggling to tell men I wanted something romantic and committed. But change was definitely on the horizon.

This adventure was a big "first," and I was building

confidence with each new experience that would lead to even bigger expansion. Now, I had to dig. Deep.

PART 2

FACING THE GREMLINS

Chapter 1

THE CATALYST FOR EXPRESSION

I VISITED SANTA MONICA, California, for the first time to see the Pacific Ocean, to hang out with friends who moved there from D.C., and you guessed it, to ascertain if a guy I liked was interested in me as more than a friend.

This guy and I lived in different states, but we met at a party over the holidays. We texted and DMed *a lot* in the months after we met. So, I decided enough was enough and offered him a chance to see me again in person.

I landed in Santa Monica and checked into a hotel. I looked around at the sun, smiling people, dogs, ocean, and cute houses. *Maybe there is something to this place,* I thought.

I explored the city the first day of my visit. I sat on the famous pier and looked out at the vast abyss of sea. I took a car to the Getty Museum to see a Leonardo da Vinci drawings exhibit, only to be more impressed by the beauty of the gardens.

The second day of my trip, though … *that* was the big day. That day I was seeing Santa Monica Guy again.

My outfit was planned. My hair blowout at Drybar was scheduled. I listened to a playlist full of upbeat pop songs as I took a quick walk that morning and my friends texted messages of support throughout the day. I glanced and smiled at my friend Jack's text, "Here we go!" as I stepped into the hotel elevator to leave that evening, my hair curled in perfect beach waves.

When the elevator doors opened, I saw my crush, sitting on a lobby bench in a blue button down and khaki shorts. As I walked over to him, the familiar gremlin narrative ran through my head: *Does he remember I walk this way?* But I kept going. He greeted me with a hug and a "Hi! Great to see you!"

We jumped in a cab and went for drinks at a cute bar that my friend recommended. As we sat down, he looked around, and said, "The nice thing about LA is all the people are beautiful looking."

I flinched on the inside but said nothing in response. The conversation moved on.

After drinks, we walked down the street to meet my friends for dinner. After dinner, the two of us headed for margaritas by ourselves on a cozy patio next door. *This seems to be headed in the right direction*, I thought as we got in the car to leave.

But I was wrong. Nobody made a move. No kissing, no holding hands, no attempt at going into my hotel room. No conversation on dating. Two steps forward and one step back again. I felt stuck in my same middle school dance story despite the changes in age, longitude, and latitude.

I didn't sleep at all that night. I was upset with myself for expecting that something sexual or romantic would happen. I was upset with him. I was upset those little gremlins still existed in my head asking if he remembered I walked the way I did.

I ruminated.

He'd made a comment that day that he knew I couldn't rent a car—which was not true—so what else did he assume I couldn't do? And why didn't I correct him? What about the beautiful people? Wasn't I one of them?

The next day, after my mental acrobatics and sob-fueled insomnia, I threw on some yoga clothes and a ballcap and walked up to Palisades Park. A strip of grass, curving sidewalks, benches, and palm trees, the park is perched on the cliffs overlooking Santa Monica pier, the beach, and the Pacific Ocean.

It was sunny and gorgeous as it usually is in Santa Monica, but I was neither on the inside. I plopped down on one of the benches, headphones in, music blaring. Definitely not pop music this time.

I sat on that bench for forty-five minutes, staring out at the ocean. And then I started to cry. A lot. Out loud and visibly.

Well, this is new, I thought. Crying in public? Was this a California thing?

I didn't try to hide it. I let the tears fill my eyes and stream down my face. There was no one around who knew me, so why not?

A stranger walked by and asked if I was OK.

I nodded. I told the stranger I was more than OK. I knew I had to take responsibility and do things differently. My college visit to the therapist and subsequent years of coaching had finally gotten me looking inward and I was taking more control.

I caught a red-eye flight home to D.C. that night. Again, there was no sleep to be had. Yes, there was more crying involved, but, more importantly, there was a lot of writing and journaling as I processed what I wanted to say to Santa Monica Guy. Specifically, I was revising a text message to tell him that I wanted to be more than friends. It suddenly wasn't enough to wait for a guy to kiss me or tell me his feelings. I had decided to be confident in what I wanted and directly communicate my feelings.

I rewrote that text probably a hundred times on the plane and had it approved by my most trusted friends. When I got home to D.C., I collapsed into bed, sent the text with a long deep sigh, and fell asleep.

Now, you know where this is headed if you're familiar with my *Los Angeles Times* headline. Santa Monica

Guy responded and told me he didn't want to date me and only wanted to be friends.

Despite that heartache, I had done a *big* thing. For the first time, I told a guy I was romantically interested in him with real words. That took confidence that hadn't been there a year prior. Proving that confidence to myself was much more valuable than having a boyfriend.

Another plus? I ended up moving to Santa Monica six months later to start my own HR advising business—likely a product of what the city had done to promote my personal development. The sunshine didn't hurt either.

Chapter 2

THE PODCAST THAT CHANGED EVERYTHING

I LOVED LIVING IN SANTA MONICA. Everything about it. I spent about six months there before moving farther south to San Diego to work with a new doctor I hoped could improve my physical mobility.

One day, as I drove to an appointment with that doctor, I tuned in to a Valentine's Day podcast that my yoga studio was hosting. I've always been a huge fan of any books, podcasts, or television shows centering on romantic relationships (probably not a shocker). But this podcast was entirely different from any I'd heard before.

The podcast guests were Londin Angel Winters and her partner Justin Patrick Pierce. As I listened, I found myself leaning into my car stereo and turning the volume way up. Their conversation continued and I repeated Londin and Justin's wisdom out loud, desperately trying to commit it to memory.

After five minutes trying to remember and process all the important things they were saying, I gave up and pulled into a grocery store parking lot where I furiously thumbed observations into my phone. I was hooked.

I hit pause, rewind, repeat on that audio track about a hundred times over the next week. I also did additional research. I bought Londin's book and listened to her videos on Instagram regularly. I was obsessed. And the reason I was obsessed was because Londin talked about dating in a way I had never heard before—and in a way I found supremely relevant to my experiences.

Londin and her partner Justin's theory? We all have two energy patterns in our bodies.

The first energy pattern, "Alpha," is structured, penetrative, and focused on purpose. The second energy pattern, "Omega," receives, expresses emotions, and is focused on the body.

We all have these patterns in our bodies, regardless of gender identity, orientation, and background. We differ, though, in which one is more expressed and in which we primarily exist. The successful practitioner is agile enough to modulate between the two when the relationship calls for it.

Suddenly, it clicked for me—the reason I was struggling to show up in dating relationships as I wanted. I couldn't modulate between the two patterns.

My Alpha energy had thrived my whole life. I taught myself to relearn to walk and talk. I looked fear in the face and moved cross-country to build a business despite not knowing more than one person. After decades of hating to ask for help, I became frustrated enough to learn how to put my hair in a ponytail with one hand. (As an aside—this was immensely difficult to learn and there is a YouTube tutorial linked at the end of this book if you need it.)

I had done all these things in my life up until this point and much more. The Alpha energy that allowed me to direct myself was off the charts. I knew how to get shit done and I was good at it.

Conversely, my Omega energy, my ability to

express and receive … nowhere to be found. It was entirely missing on the scene.

It seemed, according to my newly found information, that this missing energy pattern—the ability to better express my feelings and openly receive help—was key to finding the type of intimacy I was seeking.

Once this realization clicked, I immediately drafted an email to Londin's assistant seeking help. I told her my physical disability had caused me to exist in one emotional and energetic pattern in my body—a pattern that didn't seem conducive to dating, given the results—and I didn't want to be that way anymore. I wanted to be more emotionally agile in myself and with others.

As I typed that email, the tears trickled out. I had a newfound knowledge that change could be accelerated.

So, with all my prayers and hopes gathered up, I typed. Could Londin help me learn how to show up differently?

Chapter 3

"I'M HEARING YOU DON'T FEEL SEEN"

LONDIN, THE INTIMACY COACH, responded to my email and agreed to see me. In fact, she very much wanted to help and was excited to mentor me. We set up a plan to meet weekly for an hour starting later that year. I was ecstatic.

While things were ramping up with Londin, I spent some time studying with a business coach, Randi Braun, learning how to grow my revenue and HR advising business. The Covid-19 pandemic had begun earlier that year. Because of it, I had a lot of time on my hands and became serious about developing both personally and professionally.

So, I jumped in. I had two coaches, an osteopath

I was paying for out of pocket, and I joined a matchmaking service in San Diego. All fronts were covered. I was in debt, which my self-worth didn't love, but I knew it was necessary to put me on the path toward my goals.

The coaches and doctors were highly worth the investment, but the matchmaking service—not so much. I went on in-person dates once pandemic restrictions eased but couldn't seem to connect with anyone.

I was upfront with the matchmakers about my physical disability yet managed to get paired with a hiking enthusiast who took me on a trek up and around La Jolla Cove. If you're not familiar, picture a sandy, narrow trail with nominal guardrails, enormous seals with big teeth, and crashing waves below. Maybe not the best first date for someone with limited balance, but I managed the best I could.

The Tuesday after that date, I called my business coach, Randi, for our regular phone meeting. As I always did, I started the discussion by going through my revenue tracker and outreach. I detailed the ten potential business prospects I reached out to in the previous week. "Have you received any response?"

she asked.

"No," I said, fighting back tears of frustration.

She asked what else was going on in my life. I explained I was annoyed at a current crush (separate from the La Jolla hike guy) who persisted in texting and going out to dinner with me but never wanted to kiss me or have sex. I also explained my frustration that no one in my family seemed to understand how challenging it was to build a business from scratch or how scared I was that I had no savings.

My inner workings, anxieties, and tears poured out.

Randi was silent for a bit before responding: "Emily, I'm hearing you don't feel seen—this guy isn't seeing you in the way you would like, your family isn't seeing you the way you want to be seen, and your clients aren't seeing you."

I got so furious that I wanted to hang up the phone. That couldn't be true. Surely someone had to be seeing me as I wanted. How dare she say that about the people I cared about and wanted to work with!

While I had that fiery inner dialogue, I verbalized nothing back to her in response. I was unable to say anything. I couldn't refute her statement because I knew there was some truth in it.

The call ended pretty quickly after that; there was too much for me to process.

The weeks and months progressed. As they did, I eventually stopped communicating with my crushes at the time and found clients who did respond to my emails. As my burnout faded and I brought in more revenue, things started to make sense.

Randi was right. I wasn't fully being seen or appreciated for several reasons. I wasn't asking for what I desired in relationships. At the same time, I wasn't friends with many other people who had physical disabilities, so it indeed was *a reality* that no one shared my same experiences. The bottom line was I didn't feel seen because I wasn't positioning myself to be, well, visible.

For a very long time, the actions of the men in my life reflected that they didn't want to engage with me in the same way I wanted to engage with them, but I accepted their behavior and allowed things to continue as they were. I didn't try to explain what I wanted to be different or end the situationships quickly enough. I settled. And, in accepting that status quo, I wasn't valuing myself.

Randi hit a core wound in the coaching session that day, just like that therapist I saw in college. This time, though, I bounced back and integrated my learnings quicker. I ended the situationship I was in and sought out new opportunities. I was more confident and had a greater willingness to keep trying.

Thanks to this coaching, I recognized the historical pattern of relationships where people didn't see me fully and weren't listening to my wants and needs. With that mastered, I was on to step two: figuring out what I could change in my behavior and mindset to find relationships better suited for me.

Chapter 4

I'VE NEVER HAD SEX

In Southern California, I lived in various beach bungalows that were situated in fairly close proximity to neighbors. And when I say fairly close, I mean it was obvious when someone was crying, arguing, or getting it on.

Typically, I spent my days in these bungalows with windows and doors open to let in the warm, California breeze. But not this particular day.

After months of preparation, specifically reading her book and listening to her podcast interviews, the day had finally arrived for my first coaching session with Londin.

All my romantic problems and sexless nights were about to be solved. I may have been past my goal marriage-age of twenty-seven, but I was still a respectable thirty-five.

Before the call, I ran around the house closing all the doors and windows. The neighbors were renovating the bungalow next door, so people were in and out of their yard all day, and I had absolutely *no* intention of letting these strangers listen in on my situation.

The construction was so loud, Londin could hear it on the other side of the Zoom. We greeted each other, plugged in our headphones, and proceeded to discuss my wants and how Londin could help me.

I detailed the situation of my current crush and explained my past failures. I told her about the guy I thought I was about to start dating who texted to ask if the girl *he* had started dating could come to *my* house party. I also told her about the guy in D.C. who rejected my cookie basket overture with a brusque "Please don't ever do this again."

Londin sat there and listened, nodding along. Then, without skipping a beat or requesting further detail, she asked what kind of sexual experiences I'd had with men.

Oh god.

I glanced around the room to double check that all the windows and doors were closed. I took a deep breath, and I leaned in as far as I could to the computer screen. I'd never said this out loud before...

So, I whispered, "I've never done anything penetrative."

As I spoke, I darted my eyes away from Londin. I couldn't bear the thought that she would judge me. This stranger, whom *I was paying* to listen to me—I was afraid of her judgment.

But you know who wasn't judgmental? Londin. I had been certified as a professional coach years before this session. I knew coaches were trained to hold nonjudgmental stances, but I never truly appreciated the posture until that moment.

My shocking reveal was no big deal to her. As any good coach would, she noticed I looked away and had things to say about that. But my lack of sexual history? She thought it was beautiful, and she thought a lot of men would find it beautiful, too.

My confession and her words were exactly what I needed to get moving in a positive and more confident direction. I realized that day that I had been judgmental of my path and my life history. The fact that I couldn't look someone in the eye (over a webcam!) and speak my truth was proof enough.

I was judgmental of my history because I thought it was wrong. I thought it wasn't how I was supposed to be doing life. I thought I was supposed to be having loads of sex. After all, isn't that what pop culture teaches us? And I incorrectly assumed that all others would question my worth when they learned the truth.

I had my next homework assignment: How could I get to a place where I celebrated my differences versus judged them as wrong? I started down that path by admitting the deepest of my vulnerabilities with Londin—but, to achieve the real intimacy I wanted, I would need to learn to accept and then express that truth with the men I wanted to date.

That was the next stop in facing down my gremlins; my growth was suddenly happening quicker.

Chapter 5

"WHAT'S WRONG WITH YOUR ANKLE?"

ONE GORGEOUS SUNNY DAY IN CALIFORNIA, after my mentorship with Londin had ended, I pulled my cute navy SUV up in front of my house after yoga class and prepared to parallel park.

I am a terrible parker. I always have been and likely always will be. My tires are never scuff free, and it usually takes me two or three attempts to get the car situated.

This particular time I tried to park, there was an extra layer of awkwardness: I had an audience.

As I backed up, I looked over and a cute guy in aviator sunglasses had pulled his car parallel to mine, a gorgeous golden retriever sticking its head out the back window. I suddenly became even more self-conscious about my parking.

The guy motioned to me that he was going to park in another open spot behind me once I was situated. Could it get any more rom-commy than this? But, also, what was he going to think of my parking abilities (or lack thereof)?

I attempted to back into my spot, slowly checking both the rearview mirror and listening for the back-up sensor beeps.

When I was finally in, I looked at the cars in front of me and realized I was about a foot away from the curb. Yikes. I looked over at him nervously, he gave a smile and proceeded to back up. *Well, we will see about this*, I thought.

As I gathered my things and exited my car, the cute guy escorted the dog out of his. He looked at me and said, "That worked out well."

Indeed. I smiled.

He walked over to me, and we chatted underneath these massive oak trees that always spewed out what seemed to be an unending supply of acorns. He was headed to the beach with his dog. I was headed inside to take a work call.

The dog lingered and rubbed against my leg while its owner and I chatted for ten minutes about our interests and careers. There was definitely a vibe, one of those meet-cutes everyone in LA dreams about.

When the conversation came to a natural end, we said goodbye, and I turned to walk away.

"Wait," he called after me. "What's wrong with your ankle?"

I turned around to face him. After the words left his mouth, he stood there in silence with a slight grimace. I could tell he felt awkward.

I started to speak, and he immediately interrupted to apologize. "I'm so sorry. I shouldn't have said that."

Two years before this moment, I probably would have mumbled a nicety, rolled my eyes, and thought, *Another guy who's not interested*.

But not this time. This time I had done the inner work and instead of feeling ashamed or angry, I felt compassion for somebody who wished they had handled something differently. I felt compassion because I knew he was coming from a place of respect and previously demonstrated interest in me, not from an assumption of a stereotype.

After he apologized, I assured him that it was OK and that I would rather he ask questions than assume something about me.

The tension immediately dropped, and we launched into part two of the conversation for another five minutes.

Eventually, sunset called and off he went to the beach. I've been told the sunsets wait for no man regardless of how attractive the woman is. Such was the case.

The next day, I went out to my car. There was a scrap of paper under the windshield wiper. He had left his phone number and a note asking me out.

Needless to say, I didn't need yoga class to clear the stress and anger from my mind that day. That little handwritten note did it.

We went out for drinks and appetizers the next week. One of the first things he told me as we sat down under the twinkling lights of an outdoor patio was that he was nervous to leave the note on my car. He admitted that he rewrote it about five times.

The conversation pretty quickly progressed to our

sexual history and interests. The speed at which we got there was new. As was my response.

A year prior, during the pandemic, I had been on a Zoom date (which I truly hope I never have to do again), and I lied when my date asked about the duration of my last serious relationship.

This time though, I had no trouble being honest about my lack of history. The inner gremlins had been banished. I had put in the work. I was more confident, and I knew how to correct my inner monologue when old stories of unworthiness emerged.

His reaction to my lack of sexual experience? A little different from Londin's.

He suggested I sleep with everyone possible from that point forward, which to his disappointment, I didn't. Also, probably the reason he didn't ask me out again when a car make-out session was as far as the night progressed.

But I didn't care.

I had made real progress over the historical BS: the stereotypes, the assumptions, my shame demons, and my internal narrative. That progress was what I cared about; not having sex with just anyone. I had done too much work on myself to go that route at this point.

I've been told the emotion of shame likes to cover up. It likes to hide. However, I wasn't hiding my truth or myself anymore. And now, it wasn't just my coach who knew my secrets. Beach Guy was in the loop.

Chapter 6

"HAVE YOU EVER FELT LIKE A VICTIM?"

SHAME IS THE FEELING that you have done something wrong. Or, as my friend and psychotherapist Michael Appleton told me, shame is the response you feel when you've done something "morally objectionable."

I did nothing wrong or objectionable in having a brain injury. The injury was something I couldn't control. Likewise, I did nothing wrong by not having a boyfriend or sex in college. And yet, I felt shame around all these realities because of our societal narratives.

The sexual shame I felt was on the way out the door. Londin and the Beach Guy confessional had made sure of that. And I continued to slap that shame gremlin upside the head whenever it popped up in my subconscious.

There was still a little work to do regarding my relationship with my physical disability and how I felt about that piece of my identity. I had done inner work around it, but I hadn't fully shared my thinking on it with others.

But that "first" was about to happen: I met Brewery Guy and asked him to a party.

Brewery Guy also had a gorgeous head of hair. Actually, better than John Stamos Guy from D.C., if you can believe it. (And yes, the pattern of my preferred physical type of man is staggeringly consistent.)

All my friends at the party were quite impressed. They worshipped his hair, too. As they chatted and drank beer inside, Brewery Guy and I walked outside to find a couch and a large TV showing a basketball game.

We sat down, side by side.

At first, I was very concerned that I was leaning back too far. Seconds later, I was concerned I was leaning too far toward him. *Calm down. Breathe.* I tried to remember what Londin had taught me about being comfortable in my body and staying out of my mind.

A few minutes later, he got up and tried to adjust the position of the TV. He almost broke it and one of the brewery owners came out and asked us not to move it.

Suffice to say, between the two of us, this was a lot of awkwardness for the first time together on a couch.

Regardless, we talked. I opened up about my disability and having a brain injury as a young girl. As I shared on a more intimate level than I ever had before with a crush, he suddenly interrupted to ask: "Have you ever felt like a victim of your disability?"

What a question. And from someone who didn't have a therapy license or coaching certification. I couldn't believe it. If I wasn't awkward before, I was definitely now out of my element.

I bit my lip, looked down, and took a deep breath. My thoughts were racing.

This wasn't me telling a trusted coach about my shame and emotions, this was someone I wanted to ... ya know. This was next-level John Stamos.

I looked down at my lap considering my options, but then I looked right back up at him, straight in the eyes, as Londin had taught me.

I told him I had never felt like a victim of my disability in my professional life, but I had felt like a victim of it in my personal life.

And I didn't stop there.

I told him I felt like a victim in my personal life because the shame monster that I'd kept hidden away for years was that I had never had a boyfriend, which up until about six months prior to this interaction, I blamed on my physical disability.

Peak awkwardness. It had become a *Shrinking* meets *The Sopranos* therapy session, which was definitely not what I'd hoped for that couch.

But again, as with my other stories, that's not important.

What's important is I could have shied away from that question and life would have gone on. But I didn't shy away.

Instead, I charged straight into it and my life expanded exponentially, because I was vulnerable with a deep wound in a way I hadn't been brave enough to share before.

In that moment, I showed myself I had overcome

my pattern and learned not to hide my truth. I was no longer hiding behind the walls I built as a child, afraid to express myself for fear of what others might think or do. I was sharing the truth that had historically caused my shame despite what Brewery Guy might think.

Was it awkward? Definitely. Was he ready for that level of intimacy when he asked the question? Maybe not. I don't know.

The thing is, though, if we don't talk about the things we feel awkward about, they aren't going to get any better. We will actually feel worse about them the more we bottle them up.

And yes, Brewery Guy and I were awkward at that moment, but him asking the question and me being willing to answer with honesty signaled a big step forward for me—I had built the needed emotional skills that had held me back from the intimacy I'd desired for over twenty years.

Things were finally moving in the direction I wanted.

Chapter 7

"HOW WILL YOU KNOW WHEN YOU ARE LOVED?"

In one of our last sessions together, my intimacy coach, Londin, asked me, "How will you know when you are loved?"

At the time, I struggled to find an example with a romantic interest, but a different answer did come to mind. I told her about my maternal grandmother, Murph, who when I went to college, sent me can openers and wine openers that you could use with one hand.

I never asked for them (or frankly even knew they existed) but she instinctively knew that they would be a help, so she sent them to me without any prompt every few years. I loved her tremendously for that and much more.

Londin sat in silence, listening to the can opener story, and waited as I searched for another example of how I would know I was loved. I desperately wanted to identify a guy I had had a crush on who treated me with the level of love I craved.

But I kept coming up empty. Certainly, there were verbal affirmations and physical touch here and there, but did I feel like any guy (other than my dear friends) truly ever loved me for the real me? No.

So, I pivoted. I told her about a situation where I knew I wasn't loved—with a guy who I knew wasn't the right fit for me.

Years prior, I was cooking dinner for a date. We stood in the kitchen drinking beers and chatting when the oven timer went off. I grabbed a mitt, popped open the oven door, and pulled out my casserole. It was baking in a heavy Pyrex dish that I extracted with one hand and placed—shakily—on the range above. Very shakily. Like one shake too many and we would have been ordering pizza.

I yanked the oven mitt off and pulled out the bowls, placing them on the counter next to the dish. I plucked a serving spoon from the drawer and scooped the chicken-noodle-veggie thing I'd made, dripping sauce on the counter because I was unable to hold the bowls level with the dish.

My love interest just stood there and watched. He didn't lift a bowl to mitigate the drippage or say, "Allow me," and scoop the slop for us. He stood there and drank his beer and watched me struggle.

I relayed the story to my coach and added, "I'll know I am loved when someone steps up to help and acknowledge me and I don't overtly have to ask."

Growing up, I never asked for help. I was scared to ask because I felt it made me look weak and needy. One of the biggest stigmas people with disabilities face, in my experience, is being underestimated, infantilized, and perceived as in constant need. I did *not* want to give anyone further reason to put me in that box. Therefore, as much as I secretly longed for help opening a door when I was carrying a cup of coffee or my laptop, I made double and triple certain I could do it on my own.

I found a way to type with one hand on a standard keyboard. I found a way to zip my dress with one hand come hell or high water.

I found a way to move my things into a fourth-floor college dorm room without an elevator. And yes, before my Grandma started sending those thoughtful gifts, I tried my damnedest to cut an onion with one fully mobile hand. (Or skipped trying onion-related recipes entirely.)

This over indexing on independence became the cement in the childhood walls I built around my emotions. It held everything in place. I didn't ask for physical help because I didn't want to be stereotyped. And I didn't share my emotions with anyone because I couldn't manage the depth of pain and rejection associated with owning them.

I arrived at two conclusions in this final coaching conversation with Londin. First, I should practice asking for help as the next step in my personal growth journey. We all need help—disabled and non-disabled—and that's OK. Two, if I could find someone who understood me enough to anticipate what assistance (whether physical or emotional) was welcomed, that would be deep love.

A few years after this conversation with Londin, I was walking to trivia night with a crush. I'm a master at trivia and have loved it since college, so I was quite excited.

This guy and I had known each other for a few months.

In the course of our getting to know one another, I had never complained to him directly about my physical abilities with curbs or steps, but I had toppled off his stairs while making an attempt at a romantic gesture.

Let me elaborate. I had a holiday gift for him and I wanted a surprise delivery, so naturally my plan was to drop it in his mailbox and run away before he could see.

His apartment had four steps up to it and no flipping handrails.

No problem, I thought. Only four steps.

So, I bounded up the steps, a few weeks before our trivia outing, to drop my gift in his mailbox. After depositing it, I tried to gracefully (and quickly for fear of being discovered) step off his top step and onto the ground with my weaker leg.

Step off I did.

Gracefully? No.

I immediately collapsed and somersaulted onto the ground because my weaker leg wasn't used to holding all my body weight.

I didn't hurt myself and, as it turned out, I actually took great pride in that topple because I stood back up on my weaker left foot instead of my stronger right. In doing so, I broke a physical pattern (a pattern I had learned from that PT who kept pushing me over) and I relayed the story to my crush afterward, like a badge of honor.

Fast forward to the night we headed to trivia. He parked the car, we got out, and walked across the street.

As we approached the opposite sidewalk, I prepared to take a rather big step up to the curb. He looked over at me, smiled, laughed, and said, "What's up with this place anyway? Why don't they have any curb cutouts around here?"

I smiled back and laughed. I had found something special.

I knew at that moment that I was seen, that I was loved for exactly who I am, and that I didn't need to worry about hiding any part of me. I knew this person was someone who loved me because he knew the exact help I needed and the exact help I didn't need.

The curb wasn't super tall, so I didn't need his arm. He had seen me step up on curbs like this many times, but he also knew it required more energy and balance.

He didn't underestimate me or think I couldn't make the step, but at the same time he noticed the world wasn't set up for someone who walks like me. In acknowledging that, he gave me a beautiful moment of emotional intimacy that I didn't know I needed. He anticipated my needs. Like my Grandma did.

After years of struggle, I had banished my little gremlins and previous feelings of unworthiness to the back corners of my mind. I was able to share my full self, and I was finding the level of intimacy I desired. Yes, there was still a world to reckon with that was not set up for (or always thoughtful of) people like me, but I had become equipped to handle that reality more confidently because I wasn't allowing my past stories to lead my present narrative.

Hiding parts of myself was no longer a thing. Instead, I confidently encouraged my romantic interests to see all aspects of my identity, desires, and abilities—whether falling off steps or dominating at trivia. And because of that, I was also better able to recognize the type of men I should build relationships with—those who would love me for who I am.

My authentic full self—who I am and what I want—leads my life now.

I still haven't had a "boyfriend," but in my quest to find one, I discovered something much more important. I discovered why I love all aspects of myself as well as the path I've navigated. And why others should too.

TAKEAWAYS

TAKEAWAYS

As I mentioned in the introduction, I limited the sharing of my learnings in Parts 1 and 2 of this book to allow you to spend time with my stories and form your own reflections about how they relate to your life.

That said, over the years, I have developed a robust skill set for building confidence and thriving in intimate relationships.

These skills are not always taught to us by our schools, communities, or family units. And even when taught, what we learned back when may not be relevant today because of how fast our world changes.

For these reasons, in this final section, I'm including further takeaways and suggested skills for different readers. Please take what works for you and disregard the rest. As my friend, Gio, says, "You do you."

TO THE HATERS

I HAVE TWO HOPES FOR YOU.

First, even if you don't currently have a physical disability, you will be affected by one in your life. When physical disability manifests through an injury, accident, or random occurrence, it can cause major questioning of one's identity. As I did, in a matter of hours, you could go from being able to throw a baseball with your left hand to not being able to lift your arm at all.

The person you are dating, friends with, partnered with, or the child of will likely experience a physical disability during the course of your relationship, whether short-term or lifelong. You might too.

People are in accidents, they get cancer, they have brain injuries, and they experience illnesses. Those moments and times in our lives are not easy and they are more frequent than we would like to accept.

I did not have the tool kit I needed to thrive in those first moments and handle what followed. From my knowledge of people in similar situations, most of them didn't have the skills they needed either.

One day you will not be able to run or play a sport as well as you once did. One day you may use an assistive device to walk. How do we prepare ourselves emotionally and mentally for those changes, those inevitable chapters? As someone who had to handle them at a much younger age, it is my first hope that these stories help you better consider that future transition.

My second hope is that, after reading these stories, you now understand that my inner narrative regarding my sexual history and disability was not only wrong, it was harmful to my sense of self. And, unfortunately, disabled or non-disabled, too many of us hold (or have held) similar perspectives around self-worth.

One of the email responses to my February 2022 *Los Angeles Times* column was from someone who shared with me that "[they] too never found love because putting yourself out there [in] this day and age is tough due to constant judgments about every single thing."

We all fear constant judgments will come if we show our true selves. We are all afraid there are deal-breakers to our lovability. And many of us fear that our physical differences will cause us to be excluded from experiences that fulfill us.

Processing my emotions, spurred by the perceived deal-breakers and real obstacles in life, helped me be happier. We can't change the inhibiting realities in this world overnight, but we can learn to better deal with them. I truly hope that reflecting on these stories gives you one new tool to do that.

TO THOSE PURSUING INNER GROWTH

As I WROTE THIS BOOK, the building next door to mine in New York City was being demolished to make way for new condos.

If you'd assessed progress from the street, four months into this project, you would've assumed the team had just started work. New scaffolding wrapped the building, but the brick facade remained intact. From the outside, not much was different.

But from my window above, the story changed. The roof was gone. Inside, workers had stripped away doors, windows, and debris. Four months of work had clearly taken place—just not where a passerby could see it.

The progress I made on my self-worth, and the progress you want to make on yours, is not dissimilar from this building.

Improvement takes time.

My favorite SoulCycle instructor, Lamar, tells us to focus on getting one percent better each class. It's that straightforward. One percent better. You don't have to get ten percent better: just one.

If you are currently experiencing shame, fear, or any unhelpful emotions and want to get unstuck, I have two takeaways for you.

Number one: Get one percent better each day—whatever that means for you. Send the text to the person you want to be more than friends with. Ask that person at the gym for their number. Tell a scary truth to a coach or to a journal. Try again after a rejection.

Small steps like these are all that's needed to dismantle old walls, brick by brick.

Just like with the old building next door to me in a busy Manhattan neighborhood, you can't bulldoze everything one day and have a new structure up the next (as much as you or I might like to). So, start small. At first, it was very hard for me to express my romantic interests to someone in person, so I expressed them over text and progressed from there. I got one percent better. And even if onlookers couldn't see my progress, I knew I was growing.

Takeaway number two: Even once you've demolished your old building and, likely, the asbestos-filled walls within yourself, don't expect your shame, anger, and old stories never to rear their ugly heads again. In her book *Big Magic*,[*] author Elizabeth Gilbert talks about the "and" space that fear and creativity hold in life.

They coexist. It's not one or the other.

Gilbert doesn't allow fear to drive her decisions, but that doesn't mean fear fully exits the building. It's always there lurking. And, actually, helping you improve.

Just the same—my past feelings of shame and current feelings of confidence coexist.

My past stories and unhealthy talk track are always going to be in my body to some degree, causing me to be hesitant or triggered about certain experiences. Yours will be, too.

The question to focus on, though, is: Who do you let run the show for your decisions? The past self or the present self? (Hint: Keep striving for the present.)

---

* Elizabeth Gilbert, *Big Magic: Creative Living Beyond Fear* (Penguin Publishing Group, 2016).

TO THOSE LOOKING FOR ROMANTIC LOVE

Given I have spent most of my life in your shoes, I have many thoughts for you but have condensed them here to two major takeaways.

First: The Power of Self-Awareness.

In my former consulting career, I went into workplaces and taught people how to develop emotional intelligence skills.

Emotional intelligence is the ability to understand and manage your emotions as well as those of others. Many models of emotional intelligence exist, and every single one of them starts with self-awareness. The skill set required to be a romantic partner, who someone would want to date, also starts here.

Self-awareness is knowledge of yourself. How am I showing up? How am I communicating and reacting? When am I getting triggered? Are there patterns here?

It may take decades to develop deep self-awareness (it did for me), but trust me, it's worth it, so keep going.

There are two components to self-awareness that help me better thrive in intimate relationships: 1) Understanding what I want in a partner (behaviors, values, and communication style).

2) Knowing how I act (and catching myself when I don't act) in alignment with what I want.

My intimacy coach, Londin, was pivotal in helping me figure out the first component.

Now, I can quickly recognize the type of man I want to date based on his response to my authentic expression and his commitment to spending quality time with me (in person and over the phone). Having that clarity has given me a lot of confidence in my actions and I highly recommend you spend time reflecting here, if you haven't yet.

While you do that, let's chat about how journaling helps me with the second aspect of self-awareness.

I've wanted, and still want, a committed romantic relationship. To be successful in achieving that goal, I figured out that I needed to work on better expressing myself. My journals have served as a tracker of my progress and missteps toward that goal.

When I look back at my journals, I see Emily 1.0 (as I call her), showing up in dating relationships with shame, fear, and a story that things never worked out. She couldn't express her emotions because of her pain. I can see those behaviors, which are not conducive to successful romantic partnerships, clearly outlined in my interactions in my twenties. I was not aware of what I needed to do to reach my goal or act in alignment with it.

If I continue to read my journals, though, I then see an Emily 2.0, who started to express her emotions in her early-to mid-thirties once she realized a missing piece to her success. Her communication was still grounded in the BS of old stories, so it wasn't always easy or clear, but she did act with more alignment.

As I reach the near past in my journals, I lastly find Emily 3.0, who knows how to manage herself to rise above the BS when she feels it and can communicate in a way that serves her and the other person effectively. Her skills may not be 100 percent effective all the time, but they are pretty close.

Being aware of these iterations of Emily has been a game changer. I'm clear on what behaviors help me move toward my goals—and which ones don't. I'm also able to quickly catch myself and course correct when I start showing up again as 1.0 or 2.0.

If you don't already journal, I highly recommend it as a way to grow your self-awareness skills. I journal the answers to a series of questions every day, which are included on the website linked at the end of this book. Please feel free to borrow them if they serve you. And regardless, please pursue that self-awareness.

Phew. That's your first takeaway.

Don't worry, your second takeaway is much more concise: Don't believe everything you see on TV.

If you are looking for committed, romantic love, please try not to fixate on the idea that you're missing out by not having sex.

The idea that everyone is having fantastic sex all the time is one of the lies our dominant societal norms and Hollywood like to tell us.

I didn't have sex for a long time and even once I had oral sex, I didn't go any further for a long time after that. That was my choice, and I am very happy with it. I wasn't always happy with it, but I am now so relieved I held my ground and waited for men I really trusted.

If you want to have sex with a different partner each week, go for it. However, if you don't, please know you are not the only one out there in that situation. Figure out what you want, go at your own pace, and don't worry about your life adhering to how others define sex or relationships.

That approach is the source of true confidence.

TO PARENTS OF CHILDREN WITH PHYSICAL DISABILITIES

As recently as 2021, a TikTok trend went viral when a group of teenagers decided Helen Keller couldn't be real because they didn't believe one person could be deaf, blind, and successful.*

Similarly, in 2022, disability advocate Molly Burke appeared on *The Daily Show* and told Trevor Noah that people frequently send her messages challenging the fact that she is blind. People believe she can't be blind because she is too educated about her condition.†

---

* Rhiannon Lucy Cosslett, "Helen Keller: Why Is a TikTok Conspiracy Theory Undermining Her Story?," *The Guardian*, January 7, 2021, https://www.theguardian.com/books/2021/jan/07/helen-keller-why-is-a-tiktok-conspiracy-theory-undermining-her-story.

† Molly Burke, "Dispelling Misrepresentations of Blindness,"

Representation of authentic stories from writers and professionals with disabilities is more important than ever. If we don't elevate stories of people with disabilities at school and in our homes, we aren't giving children the education they need to challenge the conspiracy theory that Helen Keller might not be real. And we owe them that.

When I was a little girl, I tracked the different Hollywood awards shows on a paper calendar. An hour prior to the red carpet start time, I would be on the couch in front of a television, excited and ready to go.

Right after I turned fourteen, I watched Gwyneth Paltrow—resplendent in that gorgeous pink gown—win the Oscar for Best Actress and thought to myself, *When is someone who walks like me going to be up on that stage?*

No one who walks like I do won an Oscar that year and they still haven't.

The actor Viola Davis defined my childhood frustration in a segment on *The View* when she reminded us that representation is important because "you need

---

interview by Trevor Noah, *The Daily Show*, July 26, 2022. https://youtu.be/dbNDmY1-vSs?si=ce0AheqkbOdaOptf.

to see a physical manifestation of your dream."*

I didn't have that physical manifestation as a child, but your child can.

Takeaway number one is to find role models who have personal experience with disability to share. Whether that's television actors, professional mentors, historical figures, or community leaders, find them and introduce them to your child.

Likewise, find peers with disabilities for your child. I didn't have any friends with physical disabilities growing up and into my young adult years. And that absence was a mistake.

The person I value the most in my life right now is someone who experienced the same leg length discrepancy I currently have. Meeting him was life-changing in the most positive way imaginable. He lived the same reality I live, understands me on a very deep level, and as a result, I trust his advice

---

* *The View* (@TheView), "@violadavis discusses the importance of representation: 'There is something about seeing someone who looks like you that makes it more tangible.' 'You need to see a physical manifestation of your dream,' she tells #TheView," https://x.com/TheView/status/1519017295359664130

more than anyone else's. I want that same experience for everyone, so please give representation and community a consideration.

My second takeaway is to have the hard conversations you don't want to have with your children.

I know it's not easy, but whether the conversation concerns the reasons other kids stare at your child or that your child heard that people with disabilities were often murdered during World War II (as I did in the seventh grade), create the space to have the conversation, try your best, and pull in help when needed.

Our very recent past is inundated with stigma, negativity, and violence toward people with disabilities. And we do a grave disservice to the next generation when we don't discuss that historical wrongdoing with them.

An estimated 250,000 people with disabilities were murdered by the Nazis during the Holocaust.*

In the 1900s, "ugly laws" existed in the United

---

* "The Murder of People with Disabilities," Holocaust Encyclopedia, United States Holocaust Memorial Museum, https://encyclopedia.ushmm.org/content/en/article/the-murder-of-people-with-disabilities.

States to prohibit people with visible disabilities from appearing in public,* and when I was born in 1985, Americans with disabilities could still be legally discriminated against in employment (as it wasn't until 1990 that the Americans with Disabilities Act passed).†

This history and the continued physical and emotional violence perpetrated on people with disabilities are horrific.

I know we don't want to talk about this reality, but we have to talk about it if we want anything to improve. And, while none of our systemic problems and attitudinal barriers will be solved overnight, you can make a difference for your child by being honest about hate and how to handle it.

---

* Ainsley Hawthorn, "Illegal To Be 'Ugly'? The History Behind One of America's Cruelest Laws," *National Geographic*, August 9, 2024, https://www.nationalgeographic.com/history/article/history-of-ugly-laws-america-disability.

† "The ADA: Your Employment Rights as an Individual With a Disability," U.S. Equal Employment Opportunity Commission, https://www.eeoc.gov/publications/ada-your-employment-rights-individual-disability.

As I write this closing, we are living in a time in the United States where people are afraid to talk about diversity and inclusion. Where some of our country's leaders are vilifying and voicing harmful stereotypes about those of us who have disabilities and other diverse characteristics.

While I hope you, as parents, have gained skills and insight regarding how to build confidence in yourselves, I hope equally as much that you have gained an appreciation for how silence, division, and shame can damage us. As parents, you are specifically poised to change that outcome for young people with disabilities, and I hope you do—by having the conversations that scare you and promoting diverse stories.

TO THOSE IN RELATIONSHIPS

If I have learned anything over the past ten years, it's that successful relationships require internal and external effort as well as a desire and ability to prioritize them.

Some years after the pandemic, I told my friend Steven, who was also single at the time, that a new friend thought I wasn't putting enough effort into dating.

The new friend had asked, "When was the last time you went out with a guy for a drink?" When I responded, "A few months ago," they scoffed and told me I should find my way to a bar, stat.

Yikes. Not helpful advice, and I told them as much.

I was putting in as much energy as I could spare to find the right partner. And rather than think the solution was to simply march off to a bar, I knew perfecting my inner self-worth game through a lot of coaching and journaling was the effort that would pay off in the end.

As I finished the anecdote about my new friend, Steven empathized with my frustration and rightly responded, “Um … yeah, we have been putting in a lot of *fucking* effort.”

He’d been doing his own inner work and knew what was up. We laughed and I felt better.

All jokes aside, though, dating and being in successful relationships take external effort—like spending time together or picking up the phone when you’re busy—and internal effort, like improving your self-awareness and how you show up for yourself and others.

I know a lot of us (myself included before I jumped on the bandwagon!) can devalue the inner effort needed to thrive in relationships. We are more interested in what’s happening externally, like how many dates we are going on or how we can avoid angering our partners.

But, if you’re really going to thrive in an intimate relationship with someone else, you also must have intimacy with yourself. You must do the inner work.

You may develop those inner skills before you get into a serious romantic relationship, as I did. Or, as many do, you may need to develop them while you are dating or partnered to someone. Either way, this internal skill development is crucial.

Esther Perel talks extensively about how one of the problems with modern dating is that we expect too much from the other person.* We expect one person to support us in the way a community of people helps an individual. We expect one person to do for us what we should for ourselves or what friends/family/church/the gym/the therapist collectively do for us.

My takeaway for those in relationships is to work on your own inner game (in addition to continuing to go out on dates, spending time with each other, etc.). Work on your inner game so you don't expect everything out of the other person.

See what emotional support you can accomplish within yourself versus depending on a partner solely.

---

* "Esther Perel: We Expect Too Much From Our Partners," August 22, 2021, YouTube video by Bqurious, 3:31, https://www.youtube.com/watch?v=gVgVJonyAu8.

I'm guessing the support you can give yourself is a lot more than you assume. It was for me.

Bottom line—continue to work on yourself as much as possible, especially if you are in a romantic relationship. Based on my experience, it will be a gift to both of you.

UNTIL NEXT TIME...

FRIENDS, I'M LEAVING YOU WITH A QR CODE that links to resources that have helped and continue to help me improve myself. The website also includes more of my content that may serve you. I invite you to check out these resources and share them widely.

As I continue to grow in my intimate relationships, I'm quite certain we will have more to talk about and I very much look forward to that.

Until then, I'm sending much love and happiness to all. I am a beautiful and valuable person because of my physical disability. And I promise that your differences make you beautiful and valuable, too.

ACKNOWLEDGMENTS

I AM FORTUNATE TO HAVE many incredible people in my life.

Thank you in particular to these humans, who showed up for me and for this book. Please know I love you all with a depth that I didn't know was possible ten years ago.

Jaji: You saw my vision for this book and helped me make it the best it could be. Thank you for your editing and strategy skills, but more importantly for your bathroom phone calls.

J: I absolutely adore you. You make me a better person, a better writer, and a more authentic Emily. Keep putting that foot down. I'm still glad it's a b'dacle and I'm a horse.

Gio: You are my biggest champion, my best friend, and my marketing guru. I wouldn't want to do any moment of this precious life without you. Put every second of our friendship in the JAR.

Andrés and Fernando: Our time together in all my cities is so meaningful to me. In particular, thank you for getting sobbing, hysterical Emily into that cab headed out of D.C. and toward Santa Monica. This book and my growth wouldn't be here without you.

KB: Thank you for being one of my best friends and most trusted confidantes. Thank you for always making time to listen and respond to my mini podcast episodes in caring and compassionate ways. I love you.

Steven and Gary: Our Culture First San Diego prep call unexpectedly got me on my right path and I have you both to thank for it. I love you both very much. Thank you for your friendship.

Coco: Thank you for being the kind and loyal human you are. I'm so grateful for (and in awe of) how you take care of me and everyone around you.

My W 4th & Jane and Pacific Court crews: Your friendship means so much to me. Thank you for loving me and helping me step into my voice.

David, Ethan, Jeff, and Scott: Thank you for being early readers of my creative work (both what made it to print and didn't) and for championing my voice and career.

Auntie: Thank you for never doubting my mission and path. Best board of directors there is.

My parents, grandparents, and family: Thank you for letting me write and create at a young age, and thank you for supporting me when I picked my pen back up.

Lamar: Thank you for seeing and pushing the athlete in me to be better.

Londin: Your coaching and teaching changed my life. My absolute thanks to you and Justin Patrick Pierce for the amazing love and energy you put into this world.

Betsy: Thank you for always holding space for me, my emotions, and my dreams.

Remington and Keli: Thank you for giving me the final pushes I needed to get started on this book!

All of the coaches, therapists, and osteopaths who helped me grow: Thank you for helping me move forward in my journey. I have learned so much from each of you about my body, mind, and soul.

My 121 Publishizer readers: Thank you for financially supporting and backing this book in the summer 2024 crowdfunding campaign. Your early backing helped this book get the attention it needed and gave me confidence to keep going.

ABOUT THE AUTHOR

Emily Goodson is an author, keynote speaker, and strategist committed to reshaping the discourse surrounding disability, intimacy, and workplace culture.

At age eight, Emily experienced a brain injury that resulted in partial paralysis on the left side of her body. After this injury, Emily faced a host of emotional and physical challenges, achieved significant recovery, and emerged empowered to educate others.

Emily's creative work has been featured in the *Los Angeles Times*. *Dating Disability* is her first book.

www.ecgoodson.com
@ecgoodson (LinkedIn)
@ecgoodson (Instagram)
@ecgoodson244 (YouTube)